Learning to Write
Persuasive Paragraphs

Frances Purslow

WEIGL PUBLISHERS INC.

Published by Weigl Publishers Inc.
350 5th Avenue, Suite 3304, PMB 6G
New York, NY 10118-0069

Website: www.weigl.com
Copyright ©2008 WEIGL PUBLISHERS INC.

All of the Internet URLs given in the book were valid at the time of publication. However, due to the dynamic nature of the Internet, some addresses may have changed, or sites may have ceased to exist since publication. While the author and publisher regret any inconvenience this may cause readers, no responsibility for any such changes can be accepted by either the author or the publisher.

Library of Congress Cataloging-in-Publication Data

Purslow, Frances.
  Persuasive paragraphs / Frances Purslow.
     p. cm. -- (Learning to write)
  Includes index.
  ISBN 978-1-59036-731-5 (hard cover : alk. paper) -- ISBN 978-1-59036-732-2 (soft cover : alk. paper)
  1. Composition (Language arts)--Juvenile literature. 2. English language--Paragraphs--Juvenile literature.
  3. Persuasion (Rhetoric)--Juvenile literature. I. Title.
  LB1576.P8755 2008
  372.62'3--dc22
                              2007012690

Printed in the United States of America
1 2 3 4 5 6 7 8 9 0 11 10 09 08 07

Editor: Heather C. Hudak
Design: Terry Paulhus

Every reasonable effort has been made to trace ownership and to obtain permission to reprint copyright material. The publishers would be pleased to have any errors or omissions brought to their attention so that they may be corrected in subsequent printings.

Table of Contents

What is a Persuasive Paragraph?

A persuasive paragraph is a group of sentences used to **convince** someone to believe or do something. It begins with a statement that is an **opinion** or belief. Then, it offers facts to support this belief or opinion. The purpose of a persuasive paragraph is to sway the reader to agree with the author. This type of paragraph may be complete by itself, or it may be part of a longer piece of writing, such as a story.

The following is an example of a persuasive paragraph about the gold rush in California.

The local miners were the luckiest. They were the first to arrive at the gold sites. Gold miners could make $300 to $400 each day in the early months of the gold rush. About $10 million in gold was claimed in California in 1849. Many of the miners who arrived at a later date went home with nothing because most of the easy gold was gone. They were not lucky.

What is the writer trying to convince the readers to think? Find the facts the author has included in order to prove to readers that the miners who lived closest to the gold fields were the ones who made the most money.

Stating an Opinion or Belief

The following persuasive paragraph is about the life of a gold miner. By saying the miners had a hard life, the writer is expressing an opinion. The writer supports this belief with sentences that state the facts.

The miners had a hard life. Camps were often crowded and full of diseases. Supplies and food were expensive. The men did not have enough to eat. Every day, they worked long hours panning for gold. It was challenging work that was not fun. The miners were often exhausted. They had to carry heavy packs.

What can you tell from the image of miners traveling to a new dig site during the California Gold Rush? Look for clues that support your belief. Make a list of your beliefs and supporting facts.

What Are Nouns?

A persuasive paragraph is usually about a person, place, or thing. The paragraphs about the gold rush are about the event, miners, sites, fortune, and California. Each of these words refers to a person, place, or thing. These words are called nouns.

Read the following persuasive paragraph about early **homesteaders**. In 1862, the United States government gave free land in the West. This was called the Homestead Act. According to the act, each homesteader could claim 160 acres (65 hectares) of land. The free land attracted people from all over the world. In the example, the red words are nouns. They refer to something or someone. Look at the photo of the early homesteaders. List some nouns you see there.

Early settlers felt quite alone. Homesteads were often miles apart. Some people felt it was too far to walk. Still, neighbors made an effort to see each other. Neighbors shared farm work. They helped each other build homes and gather crops. They ran errands for each other.

Learning about Proper Nouns

Read the following paragraph about New York State settlers. Notice the words that begin with capital letters.

*In the 1600s, the Dutch were very important. They had the greatest influence on the area known as New Netherland. The Dutch established the **colony**'s first settlement, Fort Orange, in the Hudson Valley. A year later, they built a settlement on the southern tip of Manhattan Island. They called it New Amsterdam. The Dutch also created the state's first police force and fire brigade. They ruled the area until 1664, when the British took over. Peter Stuyvesant was the director-general of New Netherland from 1647 to 1664. In 1664, Stuyvesant **surrendered** New Amsterdam to Great Britain. The Dutch should be remembered for the huge role they played in the development of this settlement.*

"Dutch," "New Netherland," Fort Orange," "Hudson Valley," "Manhattan Island," "New Amsterdam," and "British" begin with capital letters even though they are found in the middle or at the end of the sentences. These are the names of a specific person, place, or thing. They are called proper nouns. Proper nouns always begin with a capital letter.

Visit **www.peterstuyvesant.org**, and research other sites to learn more about Peter Stuyvesant. Who are the others in the picture? Their names are proper nouns.

Fact Versus Opinion

Every day, people see, read, or hear messages. Advertisements on television try to convince people to buy certain products. It is important to judge whether the message is a fact or an opinion. Persuasive messages use facts, opinions, or a combination of both to **influence** people.

Facts are statements that can be proven. They are true statements about things that actually exist or events that have really happened. Opinions are statements of belief. Opinions may or may not be supported by facts.

The following paragraph tells about the settlers' journey across the United States.

Settlers felt a sense of pride when they completed the journey to their new homestead. Often, they were discouraged by the challenges on the trail. The journey could take four to six months and involved many hardships. Settlers traveled in groups called wagon trains. As many as 100 people traveled in one wagon train. Each group chose one guide and one captain to lead the wagon train.

The first sentence is an opinion because some people might have felt differently about finishing the journey. The last sentence is a fact because it can be proven. Now, review the other sentences in the paragraph. Are they fact or opinion?

Using Fact and Opinion to Make a Statement

Read the following persuasive paragraph about Ellis Island, which was a point of entry into the United States for **immigrants** at the turn of the twentieth century.

Ellis Island was a place of tears and sadness. About 12 million immigrants passed through Ellis Island between 1892 and 1932. These immigrants came to North America in search of a better life. Some were admitted, while others were refused entrance into the United States. Those who were not accepted were sent back to the countries they came from. It was a difficult time for these people. They felt upset.

Decide which statements are opinions and which are facts. Remember to think about which of the statements can be proven.

Parts of a Persuasive Paragraph

A persuasive paragraph has three parts. The first part is the topic sentence. The topic sentence is usually the first sentence. It states an opinion. The topic sentence tells readers what the writer would like them to think or do.

Supporting sentences generally follow the topic sentence. They provide reasons to convince readers that the opinion is correct. The reasons should be supported by facts, examples, or information from experts.

At the end of a persuasive paragraph, a sentence wraps up, or summarizes, the ideas expressed in the paragraph. This is called the concluding sentence. It is usually a strong statement. Sometimes the writer uses the concluding sentence to state what he or she wants the readers to do if they accept his or her ideas.

*Women worked just as hard as men on homesteads. They ran the households and cared for the children. They cooked the meals, milked the cows, and washed the clothes. In their gardens, they grew vegetables, which they **preserved** for winter. Women also made candles for lighting their homes and soap for washing. Women of the early West had little time to rest. They often felt there was not enough time to complete their chores.*

The topic sentence is shown in red in the paragraph about women on homesteads. Can you tell which are the supporting and concluding sentences?

Which Sentence Does Not Belong?

The following paragraph does not have unity. It includes a sentence that does not relate to the main topic. Find the sentence that is out of place in this persuasive paragraph.

The boat trip across the ocean was a frightening experience. The voyage from Scotland to the United States took many weeks. Edinburgh is the capital city of Scotland. There was no land to be seen in all that time. Also, the seas were often rough, especially if the crossing was made in winter. How high the waves were! They sometimes made the boat seem very small. Immigrants had to be brave to take on such a voyage. They left their old life behind and did not know what to expect when they landed.

The website **www.ellisisland.org** has many facts about the immigrants who landed at Ellis Island. Use information from this website to write a persuasive paragraph convincing others to come to the United States or to remain in their home countries. Make sure that the paragraph has unity.

Creating Coherence

The ideas in a paragraph should flow in a logical order from beginning to end. This is called coherence. Connecting words, such as "then," "next," and "finally," help show the order of time. These connecting words are called transitions. They connect the sentences and show the sequence of events.

Other transitions can be used to describe something in order of place, such as "nearby," "above," "inside," and "at the top."

The following persuasive paragraph has coherence. It tells about Oktoberfest. The paragraph flows in a logical order of time. Notice the transitions that show the order of time.

*Oktoberfest is a popular festival in Germany. Many German people immigrated to the United States during the 1800s and 1900s. Then, they continued their **traditions** in their new home. In the 1940s, the first Oktoberfest celebrations were held in the United States. At first, these events helped the German people honor their culture and homeland. Many people had fun at Oktoberfest. Today, hundreds of Oktoberfest celebrations are held across the country.*

LEARNING TO WRITE

Put These Sentences in Order

The following sentences describe a family tradition. Can you figure out the correct order of the sentences to create a persuasive paragraph with coherence? Look for clues to the correct order.

A. A family recipe is a thing to be treasured. When my great-grandmother left Poland many years ago, she brought with her a recipe for potato pancakes. It was not written down. It was only in Great-grandmother's memory.

B. Now, my mother is going to teach me how to make this family recipe.

C. When my grandmother married, Great-grandmother taught her how to make these special pancakes.

D. Then, my grandmother passed the recipe on to her daughter, my mother.

E. I am very lucky to be part of this tradition.

Tools for Paragraph Writing

What did you learn? Look at the questions in the "Skills" column. Compare them to the page number in the "Page" column. Refresh your memory about the content you learned during this part of the paragraph writing process by reading the "Content" column below.

SKILLS	CONTENT	PAGE
What is a persuasive paragraph?	gold miners	4–5
What are nouns?	Homesteaders Act, New Amsterdam	6–7
What is a fact? What is an opinion?	wagon trains, Ellis Island	8–9
What are the parts of a persuasive paragraph?	the life of woman settlers	10–11
What are the four types of sentences?	homesteaders	12–13
What is unity?	immigration	14–15
What is coherence?	cultural celebrations	16–17

Practice Writing Different Types of Sentences

Look at the drawing of Mormon pioneers pulling handcarts as they travel to Salt Lake City, Utah.

The first people of European ancestry to settle in the area now known as Utah were the Mormons. Mormons are members of the Church of Latter-Day Saints. This is a religion that was founded in the United States in 1830 by Joseph Smith, Jr. In 1847, Mormons migrated to Utah from Illinois after a disagreement with the government. Many thought the new land would never grow a crop. The desert land was dry. No one else wanted to live there. However, the Mormons worked hard to sow the land. Over time, it became a great place to live.

Write four sentences based on the image. Two of the sentences should include an opinion. The other two should include facts. The four sentences should be a telling sentence, an asking sentence, an exclaiming sentence, and a commanding sentence.

Put Your Knowledge to Use

Put your knowledge of persuasive paragraphs to use by writing a paragraph about what you think life might have been like for a settler or early immigrant.

Here is a photograph of an early cowboy. The paragraph about cowboys and ranching has a topic sentence, supporting sentences, and a concluding sentence. The sentences flow in a logical order and are related to each other. There are many nouns throughout the text.

*Life on a ranch was exciting. Ranchers raised **livestock** to help feed the townspeople. They also tamed horses. Cities and towns began to grow quickly in the mid-1800s. The ranching industry grew. Tens of thousands of cowboys were hired on ranches. Cowboys enjoyed working on ranches. They fixed fences and cleaned stables. It was hard work, but cowboys thought it was worth the effort.*

Select one of the photos, and write a persuasive paragraph. List the reasons and facts that support the statement you want people to believe. As you write your paragraph, make sure that it has a topic sentence, supporting sentences, and a concluding sentence. Choose only sentences that relate to your topic, and be sure that the ideas in your paragraph flow in a logical order from beginning to end. Add variety and interest by including various types of sentences.

EXPANDED CHECKLIST

Reread your paragraph, and make sure that you have all of the following.

- ☑ My paragraph has a topic sentence.
- ☑ My paragraph has supporting sentences.
- ☑ My paragraph has a concluding sentence.
- ☑ All of the sentences in my paragraph relate to the same topic.
- ☑ All of the ideas in my paragraph flow in a logical order.
- ☑ My paragraph has sentence variety.

Types of Paragraphs

Now you have learned the tools for writing persuasive paragraphs. You can use your knowledge of nouns, facts and opinion, parts of a paragraph, unity, and coherence to write persuasive paragraphs. There are three other types of paragraphs. You can use some of the same tools you learned in this book to write all types of paragraphs. The chart below shows other types of paragraphs and their key features.

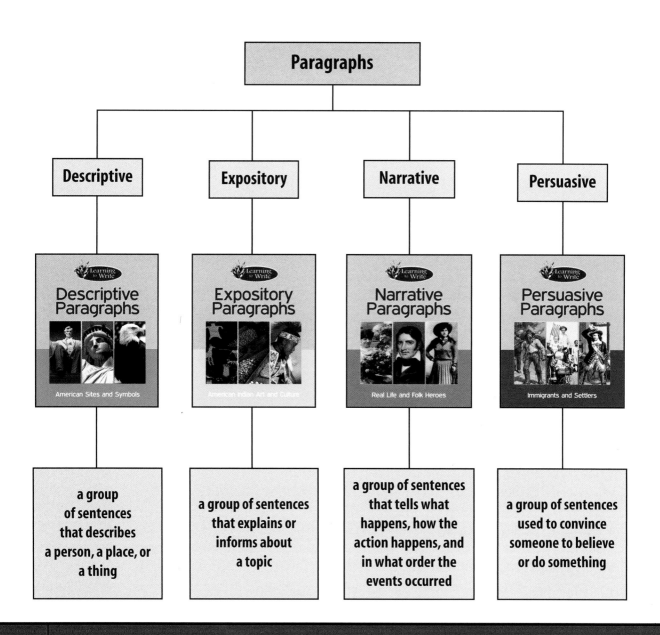

Websites for Further Research

Many books and websites provide information on writing persuasive paragraphs. To learn more about writing this type of paragraph, borrow books from the library, or surf the Internet.

To find out more about writing persuasive paragraphs, type key words, such as "writing paragraphs" into the search field of your Web browser. There are many sites that teach about early American settlers and immigrants. You can use these sites to practice writing persuasive paragraphs. Begin by selecting one topic from the site. Read about the topic, and then use the checklist on page 21 to write a paragraph.

Visit *American Heritage* to learn more about early American immigrants.
www.americanheritage.com

Harp Week Presents the American West provides firsthand accounts, images, and information about early American settlers.
http://thewest.harpweek.com/default.htm

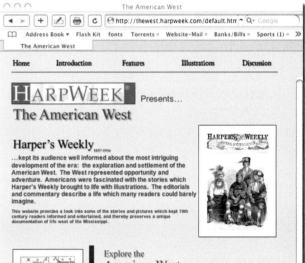

Glossary

categories: groups or classes of things or people that have shared characteristics

colony: a place that is controlled by another place; people who settle together in a place that is controlled by another country

convince: talk someone into doing or thinking something

homesteaders: people who settled on land given to settlers

immigrants: people who come to a new land to live

influence: to produce an effect

livestock: farm animals raised for sale

opinion: a view or judgment that is formed about someone or something and is not necessarily based on fact

preserved: prepared for long-term storage or kept in its original form

surrendered: gave up or handed over

traditions: customs passed down from parents to children

Index